POEMS OF
NIGHT AND DAY

Fyodor Tyutchev

POEMS OF
NIGHT AND DAY

FYÒDOR TYÚTCHEV

translated from the Russian
by Eugene M. Kayden

THE UNIVERSITY OF COLORADO
BOULDER, COLORADO
1974

ACKNOWLEDGMENT

The poems listed on pages 3 to 95, except for the four
added by the translator, originally appeared in the pages
of *The Colorado Quarterly*, in the Spring number 1971,
pages 404-412; the Summer number 1971, pages 92-120,
and the Autumn number 1971, pages 241-251. The trans-
lator is grateful for the permission and cooperation
with the *Quarterly*, published by the University of
Colorado, at Boulder.

First edition.

Distributed by *The Colorado Quarterly,* Boulder, Colorado,
80302.

Library of Congress Catalog Card Number: 73-93909
ISBN: 87081-056-1
Printed in the United State of America

Dedicated
to the memory of
Fred B. R. Hellems (1872-1929)
Melanchthon F. Libby (1864-1921)
George W. Norlin (1871-1942)

my college teachers
and friends
who made
the world's poetry
my home and heritage.

"*Who knows only his own generation
remains always a child.*"

– *GEORGE W. NORLIN*

By Eugene M. Kayden

Translations of Akhmatova, Blok, Pushkin, Baratynsky, Annensky, Maikov, Krylov, Lermontov, Mandelshtam, Nikitin, Mayakovsky, and others appeared in the pages of *The Colorado Quarterly, The Nation, Poet Lore, New Republic, The Russian Review, The Sewanee Review,* and other periodicals over a period of some forty years.

CONTENTS

INTRODUCTION

Blessed the man who lives his life
At a time of change and destiny,
Whom the exalted gods have called
Unto their feast and company.
A witness of celestial councils,
He will behold their majesty
And, godlike, in his lifetime share
Their cup of immortality.

– CICERO

OUR TWENTIETH CENTURY POETS regard Fyódor Ivánovich Tyùtchev as their first real master; they revere him as the first Russian poet of hints and allegories and still unanswered queries. Pushkin was the first to publish some of his poems in his quarterly *Sovreménnik* (The Contemporary) and Valeri Bryusov was the first modern poet to give us a biographical sketch of his life, stressing in the main his values as poet and thinker. Turgenev was the first to edit a slender volume of Tyutchev, in 1854. The poet Fet regarded him as the world's supreme lyric poet, while Count Tolstoy, who could not listen without tears to Tyutchev's pantheistic lines, held that we cannot live without his poems.

Tyutchev was born on November 23, 1803, in the province of Oryol, of an ancient and noble family of landowners known for their culture and humanitarian ideals. Russian orthodoxy, French culture, and the classics were the confluent educational forces that moulded his young life. At

xi

fourteen, he translated from Horace. He entered Moscow University in 1818, and, when he was graduated three years later, he went abroad, where he soon entered the service in the Russian Embassy at Munich. He married into an aristocratic, intellectual Bavarian family, the Countess Bottmehr. His home in Munich became a social center for men of political affairs, philosophy, and letters, among whom were Heine, Schelling, and the novelist Turgenev. It was not before 1844 that Tyutchev returned to live in Russia; in St. Petersburg, as in Munich, men and women gathered about him, fascinated by his brilliant wit and conversation. From 1857 almost to his death on July 15, 1873, he occupied the post of chairman of the Foreign Censorship Board.

Tyutchev is a poet for the few; in fact, he is a miser among poets. A small volume of about two hundred original poems is all that he left, —brief in thought, circumspect in their strict economy, but free and far-glancing in their utterance. Sensuous and evocative in the expression of ideas, his art has reserve in splendor and opulence; he traces with precision the one significant descriptive detail. Tyutchev is a lyric poet seafaring after truth. Every feeling in him is one and organic with reason, and every difficult idea is bound up with sense and memory. He feels the cool reality of earth. Man is but the dream of nature, her "thinking reed". He hears the primitive hymns of nature issue wild out of night and wind. At the heart of the world's seeming sublimity and order, he feels chaos stirring, — eternal rebellion under the cover of divine governance and law. The world is not finished, and never shall be. Chaos, negative infinity, is the deepest essence of the universe; madness and demon-like revolt are stirring in its dark abyss against the cosmic powers which would hold fast in eternal bounds the creative forces of nature. Platitudes may mumble of moral beauty and final order that have come out of chaos, of evolution sweeping gloriously onward and upward; but, in reality, night and chaos are more sovereign than day and law. Nature will not forget the titanic struggles of the past, for night was long before day, and night still holds the secret of existence. At night we may hear "the flaming chariot of first creation" moving through the heavens; in the wind, the narrative of struggles past.

And woe, too, unto him who is without sleep, peering out on the night! In the very heart of man the poet heard nature's chaos recounted — in sin, weariness, jealousy, and in revolt against order and duty. The world of matter, in creating conscious man, achieved reconciliation in reason. But modern man in his fulsome praise of reason, by taking himself at nature's evaluation, fell into an exaggerated materialism and a belief in well-being as the end of life. Living in a generation that believed with Hegel that every object was part of an endless mutability of things testifying to the harmony of one Immortal Idea, a generation that interpreted life as inevitable and regulated evolution, Tyutchev was the first Russian of his day who rebelled at the ascendancy of science in human life. Man cannot subject life to reason, mould it into an ideal pattern of existence, and give final shape and meaning to the dark striving forces. Nothing is gained for the living soul even when demonstrative knowledge is taken to the farthest edges of conscience, for the human will is mystic, and in life, in true progress, man must conceive himself free to act. Fortunately the poet did not resort to epithets about supernatural intuition and all such displays of intellectual sterility. He knew that there was no achievement without reason and self-control.

However, he would not make scientific discipline the end of existence. As reason came out of physical nature, so out of the heart of humanity will come the new synthesis and man's oneness in the spiritual principle.

It was, therefore, the historic mission of Russia, — and this is the final link in Tyutchev's cosmic philosophy, — to reconcile the contradictions of the world and to regenerate society by her power of compassion and humanity. Therefore, on the background of Russia's poor and hungering villages Tyutchev distinguished the moral beauty of the peasant who sees in Christ a poor suffering man like himself; and the greatness of the Russian people who believed in freedom, not in order to dominate others, the freedom to sin, but in order to live a life shaped by the spiritual will. He listened to the tumult of the world's highways, and he felt that modern civilization and our learned vanity have also served to disguise the original, fundamental truths, the wild heart of living things. In the unmethodical intelligence and compassion of Russia he perceived the future union of reason and humanity. He thought that the true philosophic poet, like the true artistic philosopher, is the man of the future whose multiplex nature acts as a single, organic, constant force; that in him, the threefold processes of thinking, seeing, and feeling cooperate synchronously in the work of intellectual, religious, social creation, — for the common welfare of man and society.

Yet, in his faith in his own people, there was no disdain for other nations, no vaunting of tribal virtues. Tyutchev knew that deep in the Russian soul there was also a demon of passive anarchism infecting it with a careless attitude towards work and society, a principle which hindered achievement.

Russia, he said, is not yet covered with the seamless white mantle of Jesus. But it is dawn, "silence sensitive and deep." Russia sees the world afresh. Russia evaluates her experience according to the expectations of youth and of creative generous impulses instinct with brotherhood and justice. Tremulous and eager, heart beating high, Russia now stands on the threshold opening upon the Great Adventure. A moment longer, and "a joy will sound on land and sea."

The duty of the intellectual, be he poet or physicist, is to make his specialism a bridge from the particular to the universal, from the "dream" to the "reality" of life, from egoism to God, — for our understanding and control of the world we live in. To make effective the Great Adventure, we dare not remain aloof in our private little ivory towers, hoping to keep our freedom in our isolation.

Tyutchev was a universal lyric poet who fused into one the "dream" and the "reality" of everyday life. His poetry was the magical spring and joy of *Day,* but also full of the terror and foreboding of *Night;* poetry, he claimed, was not merely the assertion that something is true and beautiful, but our readiness and will power of making truth and beauty more fully rational and socially real. He would have subscribed to William Wordsworth's statement that the poet exists because he "binds together by passion and knowledge the vast empire of human society, as it is spread over the whole earth, and over all time."

Tyutchev was orthodox and completely royalist, but his influence was widely felt in our century of revolution and democracy. We hear his voice today in Boris Pasternak (1958) as an interpreter of the Great Adventure:

No swift upheaval swelling of itself
Will clear the way for our new age to be;
Our hope – the message of a spirit kindled
By truth, compassion, and magnanimity.

Sewanee, Tenn.   E.M. KAYDEN
November 19, 1973

POEMS OF
NIGHT AND DAY

TEARS

O lacrymarum fons
— GRAY

I love, my friends, to watch with gladness
The purple of the sparkling wine,
Or fondly mark the fragrant ruby
Of clustered fruit that leaves enshrine.

And I with love gaze long when Nature
Lies drowsy with the spring; it seems
The world of being softly slumbers
In fragrance sweet and, smiling, dreams.

I love to watch the face of Beauty
Flame scarlet with the tide of spring,
When breezes stir her silken ringlets
And kiss her dimples, languishing.

But what are all the charms of Venus —
Lush grapes and roses fair that blow,
Beside the holy fount of tears,
The dew of dawning day aglow!

Celestial light lies deep within
That secret fount; its burning rays
Shine forth like rainbows in our tears,
Like solace on our troubled ways.

And when thy wings, O Angel of tears,
But touch our eyes, then mists of night
Dissolve and hosts of seraph faces
Arise to greet our mortal sight.

1823

EVENING

How quietly the far-off bell
Across the evening valley sighs!
Soft as the wings of cranes, the knell
In waving leaves and grasses dies.

Like ebbing seas, the days of spring
In sunlight glow, then slowly fade.
In mantled silence, hastening,
Across the valley creeps a shade.

1825-1827

4

A VISION

There is an hour of universal stillness, —
A wondrous hour of night and visions clear
When the flaming chariot of first Creation
Rolls through the heaven's holy sphere.

Then night grows darker; chaos broods on waters;
Like Atlas, oblivion grips lands and seas.
Alone the virgin spirit of the Muse
Feels stirred by godlike dreams and prophecies.

1828-1829

SPRING THUNDERSTORM

I love a storm in early May
When first young thunders in the sky
With rumbling wild and merriment,
Resounding, peal in azure high.

The gay young thunders roll and boom!
The drizzling rain falls on the wold.
The pearls of rain appear on threads
Of light suspended, gleaming gold.

Swift waters rush down every hill;
Each grove is twittering with song;
The chirp of birds and noise of rills
Echo the peals of thunder long.

It seems that carefree Hebe came
To feed Jove's eagle, and in her mirth
She, laughing, dashed the seething cup
Of thunderstorms upon the earth.

1828-1829

SUMMER EVENING

Down from her head the earth has rolled
The sun's great flaming ball aside;
In twilight peace the tongues of flame
Are swallowed by the ocean tide.

Daylong the sky hung close and low.
But, look! The stars are climbing high
And, with their glowing humid heads,
They lift the ceiling of the sky.

Between the sky and earth the tides
Of air are fullest; with every breeze
The breast, not burdened now by heat,
Breathes in freedom and at ease.

Through every vein of Nature flows
A tremor, quickening and sweet,
As though the waters of a fountain
Had touched with balm her burning feet.

1820's

INSOMNIA

The tolling hours in sameness drear
Their weary narrative unroll, —
In words unreal, unknown, yet clear
As conscience alive in every soul.

We hear with grieving hearts their chime
Through universal stillness swell;
We hear the muffled cries of time
And voices boding their farewell.

We judge our world's been overthrown
By some unalterable fate,
That, orphaned, we've been left alone
To cope with nature, chaos, hate.

Our life seems like a passing show,
A phantom on the verge of earth;
From dark to dark are fading slow
Our days and friends we knew since birth.

While generations of the young
Grow lusty in the sun each day,
Our age, discarded and unsung,
Must pass, unknown, in dark astray.

But sometimes, at the mournful rite
Observed by custom at the tomb,
A requiem of eternal light
Will lament our inevitable doom.

1820's

8

SPRING WATERS

Although the fields are white with snow,
The rills grow boisterous with spring.
They run, they wake the sleepy banks.
The dancing freshets shout and sing —

They shout and sing in every field:
O Spring is near! O Spring is near!
We are the harbingers of Spring
Sent forth to cry that Spring is here!

O Spring is near! O Spring is near!
Behold, with flowers gay, the throng
Of radiant and warm May days
Come in her train with joy and song.

1827-1830

THE LAST CATACLYSM

When the last hour will toll the death of Nature
All the elements will crumble into chaos:
The floods will cover then the world we know
And the face of God will brood upon the waters.

1828-1830

TIDES OF DREAM

As ocean tides the ball of earth surround,
By tides of dream the whole of life is bound;
Comes night again, upon the curving shores
The vast resounding cosmos roars.

Its voice rings urgent o'er the inland bay;
On lifted wings enchanted sways a bark.
The flood swells high and swift we float away
Into the immeasurable dark.

With starry spendor bright, the vault of night
Gazes within the deeps mysterious.
We sail, sail far, — above and under us,
The sea's abyss of blazing light.

1828-1830

DREAM AT SEA

The sea and the hurricane rocked our boat,
And, dreaming, I yielded myself to the waves.
Two infinite states of being and power
Possessed me, resigned to their will and caprice.
Around me, like cymbals, resounded the cliffs
To echoing winds and the song of the surge.
Bewildered, I soared in the chaos of sounds,
But my dream rose higher midst chaos and void;
In the magic of silence, in feverish rays,
It hovered aloft in the thundering gloom.
I fancied a wonderful realm in my dream:
Sweet grasses and roses aglow in clear air,
White palaces, gardens, fair halls, colonnades
Where multitudes swarmed in speechless amaze.
I discovered the features of peoples unknown;
I saw marvelous creatures, mysterious birds.
I moved like a god in creation on high
And the motionless universe shone at my feet.
Like a sorcerer's howling, the heave of the deep
And the growling of rollers I heard in my dream.
The swirl of the tide and the whirlpool crashed
In regions serene of my vision and dream.

1828-1830

12

THE SOUL

The soul doth yearn to be a star —
Not of midnight when from the skies
Those silver orbs, like living eyes,
Gaze on our drowsy world afar;

But of high noon when it appears
That stars, beyond the sun's vast blaze,
Shine godlike, brighter still, like rays
Unseen and pure within the spheres.

1828-1830

This symbolic poem expresses Tyutchev's humble contem-
plation of unattainable purity and perfection in life. *The Soul* is a
generalized view of man as the image of undying light of God.
The poem was a favorite of Count Leo Tolstoy because it
seemed to establish man's fathomless origin and spiritual affin-
ity in the Eternal, in words at once simple and direct. Tolstoy
disliked poetry as a rule, but he said, "We cannot live without
Tyutchev." This poem was to his mind the perfect fusion of
highest religious thought and poetic expression.

TRANQUILITY

The storm has passed. But one tall oak
Lies smouldering, by lightning slain,
And from its limbs the blueish smoke
Streams over grasses wet with rain.

The grove hums louder now with bees,
With melodies of thrush and lark,
And o'er the crest of tallest trees
The rainbow leans its shining arc.

1828-1830

14

UNTO TWO SISTERS

By chance I saw you with your sister,
And all your loveliness I read
Within her face: your shy delight,
Your tenderness, the morning light,
And grace that hovered round your head.

Today, as in a magic mirror,
Again what came to pass I know:
Your joys, your sorrows of the past,
Your youth departed, and, at last,
My love for you doomed long ago.

1828-1830

15

THE ALPS

Through the boundless azure twilight
Snow-clad Alpine mountains frown:
There the eyes of frozen giants
Gaze in icy terror down.
Haunted by some secret power
Till fair morning spreads her wings,
In the mist they slumber sternly
Like a race of fallen kings.

When at dawn the East grows purple
And the mountain peaks turn rose,
Gleaming in its crown of gold
First the highest summit glows.
Soon the lower peaks in dawnlight
Shine and sparkle till, behold,
All the summits, resurrected,
Glitter in their crowns of gold.

1830

LEAVES

Let pine trees, let spruces
Stay all winter aglow,
And lulled by the stormwinds
Sleep mantled in snow.
Like spines of the hedgehog
Pine needles are long;
And though never yellow,
They do not grow young.

We bloomed for a summer,
Light-hearted and gay,
And briefly we tarried
On branch and on spray.
For a summer, delightful
In splendor, we grew;
We dallied with sunlight
And washed in the dew!

Now birds sing no longer;
The flowers lie dead.
The meadows are hoary
And breezes have fled.
Why hang on the branches,
Grow yellow in rain?
It's gayer to follow
The winds on the plain!

O blustering winds
From over the seas,
Come, quick, and take us
From wearisome trees!

Come, quick, and take us,
We care not to stay!
Fly, fly, and bear us
Away, far away!

1830

MALARIA

I love this wrath divine! This evil I love
That flows unknown, invisible in grass
And flower, in fountains like the clearest glass,
In rainbow hues, in Rome's blue sky above.
And though sublime the same unclouded sky,
And though at ease the heart unmoved by care,
And though in trees the same warm breezes sigh,
And though sweet the rose, death lurks everywhere.

Perhaps there dwells a balm enravishing
In hues and sounds, in fragrance of the flower,
Proclaiming to the mind our final hour
Through gifts of solace for our suffering.
'Tis thus the messenger of Fate, concealed
In golden-tissued veils of day and light,
Appears upon this earth, but, unrevealed,
He keeps his dreadful coming in the night.

1830

ON THE ROAD

The sands come to our horses' shanks.
Slowly we drive until the day
Grows dark. The firs in gloomy ranks
Make one vast shadow upon our way.

Deeper, darker the woods arise.
The fields lie sighing mournfully.
Night like a beast of a thousand eyes
Gazes behind each bush and tree.

1830

LITHUANIAN PLAINS

I journeyed through Lithuanian plains,
Through level fields of sand and gloom.
From livid skies and tracts of sand
I learned a people's ancient doom.

I then recalled their doleful past,
A lifetime gripped by war and lust
When Teuton conquerors had gored
Poor peasant supplicants in dust.

I beheld with pain those desolate
Lone firtree woods, the river's flow;
I felt these ancient witnesses
Had known the times of blood and woe.

They seemed like ghostly spirits come
From borders of a world unknown;
They bore their eternal mysteries
And kept their secrets as their own.

But nature's only a silent witness
For those past days of wrong and might,
Like a lad whose morning silence hides
Dread scenes he'd witnessed in the night.

1830

AUTUMN EVENING

No evening is lovelier in brilliancy
Than this fair autumn hour! The baneful sheen
On trees of magic hues; the elegy
Of crimson leaves all languid, light, serene;
The tranquil azure of the misty skies
Above the orphaned earth of quiet sorrow;
The broken squall of a north wind that cries
Its auguries of storms upon the morrow;
The sense of weariness in wood and field,
The wistful smile of meekness and of waning, —
The smile that in a human soul, revealed
At death, shines godlike, shy, and uncomplaining.

1830

CICERO

Thus spoke the Roman orator
In days of tumult and dismay:
"I rose too late; the night of Rome
Came down while I was on my way."*
But, parting from your Rome of glory,
Upon her templed hills that day
You saw her bloody star declining,
The sunset of her splendid day.

Blessèd the man who lives his life
At a time of change and destiny,
Whom the exalted gods have called
Unto their feast and company.
A witness of celestial councils,
He will behold their majesty
And, godlike, in his lifetime share
Their cup of immortality.

1830

*The words ascribed to Cicero in lines 3-4 refer to the follow-
ing classical text: "Doleo me in vitam paullo serius, tanquam in
viam, ingressum, priusquam confectum iter sit, in hanc
reipulicae noctem incidisse." (*Brutus, sive dialogus de claris
oratoribus*, ch. XCVI: 330.)

SILENTIUM!

Be silent, live unknown! Conceal
The dreams you live, the love you feel,
And let your visions rise and die
Deep in your heart as stars on high
Die silently in boundless night.
Be silent, joyous in their sight!

How can your heart at will command
New words and forms? Who'll understand
The faith by which you live and die?
A thought when spoken becomes a lie:
Oh, do not stir the fountain-source
But, silent, drink its living force.

Be true and keep yourself at peace!
For yours the magic harmonies
And secret treasures of the mind;
Then flee the busy world, the blind
Distempered day, and heed alone
Their quiet music. Live, unknown!

1830

CHARGER OF THE SEA

Fierce charger of the sea,
Steed of the pale-green mane!
Now gentle, meek, and tame,
Then sportive, wild again!
The raging whirlwind built
Your strength in boundless space
And made your bones like bronze,
Your sinews for the race.

I love you when, headlong,
Your leap in might and pride,
Your mane athwart the storm,
Along the surging tide,
When like a trumpet sound,
Your hoofs and neighing gay
Die on the rocky shore
And glitter in the spray.

1830-1835

AS OVER A GLOWING PILE OF ASH

As over a glowing pile of ash
A parchment smokes, consumed by flame,
And as the secret, muffled heat
Devours at last each word and line,

Thus sadly smoulders every day
My life and wastes away in smoke;
Thus gradually my life dies out
In unendurable monotony.

O Heaven, heed but once my prayer
And let that flame unfurl at will
That I, without distress or grief,
May quickly flare up — and die out.

1830's

LUTHERANS, I LIKE YOUR LITURGY

Lutherans, I like your liturgy;
It is simple, solemn, and austere.
The teachings of your cold bare walls
I like: I find their lesson clear.

But mark! As one prepared to leave,
Faith waits among your people there.
She has not crossed the threshold yet
But her house is empty, swept and bare.

She waits, prepared, within cold walls;
She has not left nor shut the door . . . .
The hour has come. Pray to the Lord,
O brethren, lest we may pray no more.

1834

I CALL TO MIND A MOMENT GOLDEN

I call to mind a moment golden;
I call to mind a lovely place.
We were alone. In evening twilight
The Danube thundered in his race.

Upon a hill where, whitely gleaming,
The ruins of a castle stood,
You leaned against a mossy boulder —
A fairy in your youthful mood.

Your foot you gently rested on
A granite rock. The sky shone blue.
The sun, departing, smiled farewell
To hills, the castle, and to you.

The gentle breezes in their passing
Caressed in play your dress and hair,
And strewed wild apple petals over
Your shining head and shoulders bare.

You watched the sunset sky until
The last bright rays were seen no more.
Then twilight came. The flood resounded
Still louder on the darkened shore.

You watched the happy day depart
In unaffected pleasure, gay
At heart, while soft above us faded
The perfumed shadows of the day.

1832-1835

O WIND OF NIGHT

Of what thy wailing, O wind of night?
Of what thy rage and frantic crying?
What means thy voice, now wild and strange,
Now plaintive in the midnight sighing?
I hear thy voice of mystic grief
And woe beyond all comprehending,
And feel within my inmost being
Thy piercing cries of wrath unending.

Cease, O Wind, thy fearful chants
Of ancient time and chaos singing!
How breathless in the secret night
We listen to thy message winging,
And long to flee this prison life
Into the infinite unknown!
O wake not from their sleep the storms!
Beneath them chaos moves alone!

1831-1836

THE STREAM IN DARK,
DEEP TORPOR

The stream in dark, deep torpor
Seems hidden in solid ice,
Its light and sounds enchained
By cold in caverned death.
But the spring's eternal life
The cold cannot enchain;
Forever it will strive
To break the dead dark peace.

O teach the orphaned heart,
Overborne by wrongs and hate,
The upheaval of the deep,
The bright universe of youth:
Do you then no longer hear
The stir neath the icy crust,
The murmur of young waves,
The voice of the secret source?

1831-1836

EVENING MIST

Evening mist and chilly weather.
Is it a skylark? Bird, or sprite?
Do I dream? . . . O joyous spirit,
You, this dead late hour of night?
Joyous, lithesome strains resounding
In this late, dead hour of night,
Like a cry of shrill mad laughter,
Shook my heart with pain tonight.

1831-1836

THE WILLOW TREE

Why, O Willow, o'er the river
Do you droop your branches low
While your leaves with longing quiver
As above the flood they shiver,
Thirsting near the river's flow?

Gay, the shining river splashes
Though your branches grieve and dream:
Far the river flies and dashes,
Far in sunlight gleams and flashes,
Mocking at your empty dream!

1831-1836

TWILIGHT

Shadows blend in blue confusion;
Color, sounds, and scent subside.
Life and motion wane in darkness
Far upon a trembling tide.
There a night moth in its passing
Stirs the dark invisibly . . .
Oh, this hour of wordless longing!
I, in all; and all, in me . . .

Gentle twilight, brooding twilight,
Flow into my soul like balm!
Fill my being with thy languid,
With thy fragrant, healing calm!
In the fountain of oblivion
All my conscious life submerse!
Grant a fuller life of wholeness
Within thy dreaming universe!

1831-1836

OLD WINTER JUSTLY RAGES

Old Winter justly rages!
Her days are nearly past.
Fair Spring raps on the window
And chases Winter fast.

And now all Nature hustles
The Winter witch along;
The skylarks in the azure
Soar high with peals of song.

Old Winter frets and grumbles
At her rival angrily;
But Spring pipes even louder
And laughs out merrily.

Old Winter fumes and rages,
And scampering away,
She hurls a snowball flying
At the fair child of May.

Away with care and trouble!
Spring laves her face in snow
And, rosier each morning,
She shines despite her foe.

1831-1836

34

I LOVE THE BEAUTY OF YOUR EYES

I love the beauty of your eyes,
My dear, their play and brilliancy,
When of a sudden, in surprise,
They flash a moment fearlessly
Like lightning blazing in the skies.

But greater far your charm for me
When your eyes grow dim as in a dream,
Aglow with passion suddenly,
When tears beneath your lashes gleam
With longing dark and ecstasy.

1831-1836

HOW SWEET AT DUSK
OUR GARDEN DREAMS

How sweet at dusk our garden dreams
Enfolded soft in evening blue!
How sweet the golden moon shines bright
Upon the apple trees in bloom!

The night is vast, aflame with stars
As on the first day of Creation.
A far-off music fills the air;
The rills at night sing louder, near.

A dusky veil enfolds the spheres;
The earth lies weary, still, at rest.
Above the city, deep in slumber,
New magic voices wake at night.

Whence these unfathomable sounds?
Perhaps our thoughts, by sleep unfettered,
Behold a world unbodied, vast, unseen,
Astir within primeval night.

1831-1836

A FLUTTER WAKES
AMONG THE FIRS

A flutter wakes among the firs.
Although the earth lies sad and bare,
A breath of spring is in the air;
A dead stalk in the meadow stirs.

Though nature seems unawakening,
Insensate in her winter sleep,
It feels the tide of summer, deep
Within her swelling, and smiles at spring.

O Soul, thy sleep was long! What gleam
Of life now stirs thee suddenly?
What vision comes to comfort thee,
To kiss thy face, to gild thy dream?

The melting snows lie glistening —
How vast the azure skies above!
Is this the awakening of love?
Is this the tenderness of spring?

1831-1836

NATURE

Nature is not what you may fancy:
No lifeless image, not a copy.
She has a soul, a voice, inspired
By love and by her own free will.
. . . . *

Are leaves, are blossoms on a tree
The craftsmanship of gardeners?
What seed will ripen in the womb
By a magical or alien force?
. . . . *

Refuse to hear, refuse to see,
And, like the blind, in darkness live
If suns are only matter dead
And sea waves have no pulse or life.

Spring does not bloom in ice-cold hearts
Nor sunbeams in unfeeling souls:
The nights of glowing stars are mute
And trees are speechless in their midst.

The thunder-storms that shake the woods
And waters with unearthly tongues
Are not in fellowship your friends
Conversing in the night with you!

O never will the deaf-mutes feel
Or know the life of Nature here!
They are unmoved, indifferent
Even unto a mother's voice!

1831-1836

*The censors struck out two stanzas of four lines each. Push-
kin, as editor of the *Sovremennik,* boldly "restored" the offend-
ing stanzas with eight lines of dots. Readers naturally sneered at
the censors.

HARP OF SKALDS

O harp of skalds, for centuries in sleep
Forgotten in this nook, in silence deep!
But when the moon, enchanting all the gloom,
Shone radiant within this lonely room,
Thy wondrous chords awoke in magic sound
Like a soul's cry heard in a dream profound.

What ancient life is waking with thy strain?
What great heroic ages live again?
What songs of maidens passionately glow
With runes forgotten, silenced long ago?
And in these gardens blowing here, come they
Unseen with dancing measures light and gay?

1837

40

ITALIAN VILLA

From strife and woe it parted long ago
And fenced itself behind a cypress grove,
Its halls and porches in eternal slumber
As within the shades of Paradise.

And thus for two full centuries or more,
Enfolded in the magic of a dream,
Within the flowering vales the villa slumbered
In kinship with the sky and air.

The tender skies embrace this land at peace,
Asleep. Year after year warm southern breezes
Wing drowsily across the cypress trees,
Yet no leaf stirs nor falls in fear.

A fountain bubbles here beside the wall;
The breezes wander free beneath the arches,
And swallows twitter in their shadows. Deep
The villa slumbers; deep, the dream.

We ventured on the porch. So still the air,
So calm the dark, — beyond our life and time!
We heard the fountain murmur; motionless,
A cypress looked in at the window.

Then suddenly a tremor shook the villa
And ran, convulsive, through the cypress branches.
The fount grew still, and yet a wondrous whisper
Resounded faint as in a dream.

Darling, what evil entered here with us?
What heat of discontent if not our own?

What evil has invaded this domain
And crossed this sacred threshold stone?

1837

SPRING

Though now defeated and degraded
By struggles setting men apart,
By woes that subjugate the mind,
By every anguish of the heart
Endured, forget the yesterdays
Of cruelty and of suffering!
Who can resist the healing breath,
The gladness of the early spring?

She comes, a stranger to your prayers,
A stranger to your wrongs and grief.
She comes, immortal in her calm
And fair in every spray and leaf.
Obedient to her will and pattern,
She comes at her appointed hour, —
Indifferent, but, like a goddess,
Resplendent in her quiet power.

She walks with flowers in Creation,
Each year her first, her fairest spring!
Though other springs have come before
As winter days were vanishing,
This brightness of the sky and clouds
Glows now for this new spring alone.
No trace she finds of other springs
And flowers that were but now have flown.

No rose will mourn, no nightingale
Regrets the passing of the years,
And no Aurora weeps for days
Gone by her aromatic tears.

Not one green leaf of hers will fall
In dread of certain future doom,
But shimmers like a shoreless sea
In brightness of its present bloom.

O victim of your private good,
O mortal, cast illusion out!
Come brave and self-possessed into
This living stream of life about
You shining! In radiance of being
Cleanse now your spirit from all strife
And share with each new spring her gift —
Her godlike universal life.

1831-1839

NIGHT AND DAY

Above the spirits' secret world,
Above the void and gloom of chaos,
The sovereign gods in their great mercy
A golden-tissued veil unfurled.
We call it Day — life-giving, kind, —
This veil of blessedness and splendor,
Bringer of healing to the living,
Friend unto gods and all mankind.

Day fades away. Comes twilight pale
And darkness rends with dusky fingers
The blessed, golden-tissued curtain
And casts aside the shining veil . . . .
So vast and naked in our sight
The abyss of darkness and of terror,
We stand, unshielded, undefended,
And, in our awe, we fear the Night.

1831-1839

NEVER TRUST THE POET

O never, never trust the poet,
Sweet maid, nor call him yours above
The rest. More than his flaming anger
Fear his sublime delight and love.

You cannot make his heart your own
Through the surrender of your soul,
Nor safeguard in your virgin veil
From harm his life of glowing coal.

His fancy rules among the spheres,
But himself he cannot change or sway;
His wreath unwittingly will sear
Too soon your golden locks away.

In vain the idle multitudes
Bespeak their praise of him or blame:
Not his the serpent fang but, like
A bee, he stings and gathers fame.

His blameless hand will ne'er at will
Defile your sanctuary shroud,
But, unaware, he'll crush your life
Or bear you far beyond the clouds.

1831-1839

THE ROCK AND THE SEA

Storms at sea! Wild terror lashing,
Billows seething, roaring might
Spinning waterspouts and flashing
Toward unshaken starry height!
Is it Hell despoiling, boiling
Neath the Sea's tumultuous sweep,
Like death-flames in caverns coiling,
Flinging upside down the deep?

Long sea tides in fury, scaling
Higher as they, frenzied, roar,
Howling in the vast and wailing,
Tumble upon the granite shore.
But, serene in pride of power,
Changeless midst the storms and rages,
Stand in thy triumphant hour!
Stand in greatness, Rock of Ages!

Frenzied in their battles, raging
In their fateful wild sea-flight,
Fiercely their offensive waging,
Waves overwhelm the Rock of might.
Broken, tossed apart, depleted
From their steady, long attack,
Billows churn, retreat, defeated,
In the stream of foam far back.

Stand, O Rock, unmoved by raging
Waters and the thunder-peal!
Wait: the seas will cease their waging
War upon thy granite heel.

Torn by struggles, agitation,
Soon the storms and wailing seas,
Lulled at last, in abdication,
Neath thy heel will rest in peace.

1848

FOR LOVE OF YOU

For love of you, my dear, I languish;
I long for you in my despair;
In gloom of my remembered anguish
I worship still your features fair, —
Your features fair, remembered ever,
Before me always, near or far,
Abiding and unchanged forever
As in the sky of night — a star!

1848

In this lyric the poet recalls his love for Eleanor, the Countess Bottmehr, his first wife who died in 1838 at the age of thirty-nine. Though married a second time for nine years, he thinks of Eleanor as of a star, an ideal beyond his reach. He had three girls by Eleanor: Anna (1829-1889), Daria (1834-1903) and Ekaterina (1835-1882).

POETRY

Amidst the thunder, tempest, fire,
Amidst their boiling, swirling ire,
In flaming strife and disarray
From heaven to the earth she flies
With azure brightness in her eyes
To live among the sons of clay, —
And on the wild tumultuous sea
She pours the oil of harmony.

1848

ON A SUMMER NIGHT

On a still, warm summer night,
Still beneath a starry sky,
Field on field shine far in light,
Heavy with a dream of rye.

Deep in silence, field and wold
Slumber in the dark of night,
And their undulating gold
Glimmers in the pale moonlight.

1849

TWIN DEITIES

Twin deities, like twins earthborn,
Are Sleep and Death, remarkably
Alike as a brother and his sister:
He is more meek; more tender, she.

But there is another pair of twins,
A spendid pair in every feature, —
Alluring and inspiring fear,
Bewitching every human creature.

Born of one blood, not by mischance
They live in kinship; on fateful days
Their inexplicable mysteries
By their enravishment amaze.

Whose blood in an excess of passion,
Whose heart by many sorrows tried
Has never known your dread temptation,
Ye twins of Love and Suicide?

1850

Sleep and Death are treated as earthborn twins. In Russian,
sleep (*son*) is masculine, and death (*smert'*) is a feminine noun.

SUDDEN RAIN

In doubt, irresolute,
The sun is gazing down.
A thunderclap! The earth
Lies clouded in a frown.

A rush of warmer winds
And raindrops in a swarm.
The greening fields of grain
Shine greener in the storm.

Blue spears of lightning shine,
Cascade from cloud to cloud,
As they flash from end to end
Still whiter than a shroud.

In a whirl of dust the rain
Across the meadow flies.
Still angrier and bolder,
The thunder in the skies.

Again the fields are glad
To see the sun's shy glance.
The ruffled earth at rest
Smiles calm in radiance.

1849

TEARS OF MY PEOPLE

Tears of my people, O tears of my people!
Early and late, in all seasons, they flow,
Falling unseen, in secret, unknown, —
Endlessly falling, welling from sorrow,
Falling like rains of the autumn in darkness,
Soundless and drear, in the darkness of night.

1849

HOLY NIGHT ASCENDS

Holy night ascends into the firmament
And rolls away the golden veil of bliss,
Our day of solace and of tenderness, —
The golden veil spread o'er the black abyss.

The outward world of being like a vision
Dissolves in air, and man stands face to face,
Helpless and naked, like a homeless orphan
In gulfs of dark, unfathomable space.

He peers with his unprofitable mind,
In all the barren universe alone,
No stay nor power outside his orphaned soul
Sustaining him, no firm foundation-stone.

Then like a vanished dream the shapes of life
And light appear to him, and he forthright
Perceives his true ancestral heritage
In that inexplicable, alien Night.

1849

VOUCHSAFE, O LORD,
THY CONSOLATION

Vouchsafe, O Lord, Thy consolation
To him who, spent with summer heat,
On burning sidewalks, like a beggar,
Past gardens drags his heavy feet;

To him who sees across high fences
The shut-in lawns, the shady trees,
But cannot reach the meadow's splendor
Of soft, cool grass to rest at ease.

Oh, not for him the oaks and birches
Spread shadows on the sultry way,
And not for him the friendly fountains
Lift high their clouds of silver spray.

In vain the peaceful azure grotto
Invites, as in a haze, his sight;
The cool and dewy mist of fountains
Not him will freshen nor delight.

Vouchsafe, O Lord, Thy consolation
To him who, through the summer heat,
On burning sidewalks past a garden
Must like a beggar drag his feet.

1850

AUTUMN WOODS

Enfolded in a dream profound,
The drowsy woods fade mournfully.
All naked in the autumn weather,
Now few the leaves by summer crowned
Hang, trembling, flaming on a tree.

I watch with tender sympathy
When, breaking through the clouds on high
Against the gathered autumn darkness,
One ray, like lightning, suddenly
Splashes a dappled tree nearby.

How dear these fading trees! What tale
Of charm in woods of summer prime!
What glory gladdening the spirit
When, fading slow, so faint, so frail,
They smile to us for the last time!

1850

BARELY COOL FROM HEAT OF NOON

Barely cool from heat of noon
Glitters warm the summer night.
Storm-filled skies without a moon
Gathered over field and dune
Tremble with fantastic light.

As gloom-heavy eyes in sleep
Open sternly, so in the skies
Dread between vast lashes deep,
Blazing on their downward sweep,
Mutely flame a Being's eyes.

1850-1851

HOW CRUELLY WE LOVE OUR OWN

How cruelly we love our own
When, lashed by passion or by fear,
We ruin unfailingly the life
That inwardly we hold most dear!

You cried but yesterday in pride
And self-assurance: She is mine!
Before the year was out, what good
The triumph of your love divine?

Where now the roses in her cheeks,
Her smile of love, her eyes of light?
All these are seared by bitter tears
Wept long in secret of the night.

Can you remember now when first
You met upon that fateful day—
Her magic glance, her voice, her joy,
Her girlish laughter ringing gay?

But, pray, where is all this? How long
The dream of your eternal quest?
Alas! Like northern summer days,
Your love was but a passing guest.

A dreadful sentence writ by fate
Your love for her at last became,
Like a burden laid upon her life,
A life of undeservèd shame.

Her spirit now must suffer grief
And self-denial day by day;
Her memories alone remain,
But they, too, will in time betray.

For her the world became a waste,
Her joy in living turned to rust.
The bloom that opened in her soul
Trod down by surging crowds to dust.

What gain to her the lasting grief,
Mere ashes saved in memory?
What gain in bitter pain to languish
In tearless woe, in agony?

How cruelly we love our own
When, lashed by passion or by fear,
We ruin unfailingly the life
That inwardly we hold most dear!

1850-1851

FIRST LEAVES

O fresh young leaves! How fair
The tender, slender sprays
Are greening in the birches
And undulate in air
Through a transparent haze!

They dreamed a time ago
This golden summer light!
Now quick with life the birches
In tides of summer bright,
In their groves awakened, glow.

O fresh young leaves, in rays
Of morning gleaming green!
When breezes of the meadows
Murmur in new-born shadows,
Not a yellow leaf is seen
Upon ten thousand sprays!

1851

OUR AGE

No sickness of the flesh, our modern plight!
Our souls, denying life, are pining; grieving,
We strive in gloom for light; yet finding light,
Rebellious, we repine, still unbelieving.

Withered and spent by unbelief, the soul
Endures woes unendurable, not daring
To pray for faith, yet knowing it has no goal
Nor hope in life through days of long despairing.

Our age will not cry out in tears, nor pray,
Although we wait before closed doors in grief
For man's salvation. We do not humbly say:
"Lord, I believe! Help Thou my unbelief!"

1851

THOUGHT AND WAVE

Thought after thought, like wave after wave, —
One in their essence, a thought or a wave!
Cribbed in the mind or on the infinite ocean,
Here in their prison or free in their motion, —
Always the same in their billowing race,
Forever like phantoms eternal in space!

1851

HOW GAY THE SUMMER
THUNDERS BOOM

How gay the summer thunders boom
When a sudden overwhelming gust
Of tempest-wind with flying dust
Disturbs the azure sky with gloom,
And rushes, headlong, furious,
Upon the forest multitude!
A trembling runs throughout the wood,
Far-sounding and tumultuous.

As if crushed beneath an unseen foot
The forest giants bend, resigned,
In fear before the rushing wind,
And mutter in their tribal moot.
But midst their sudden wild dismay
The birds pipe louder, and somewhere
Floats slowly, spinning in the air,
One yellow leaf upon the way.

1851

PREDESTINATION

O Love, thou art, so runs tradition,
The fusion of a soul with soul —
Their intermingling and fruition,
Their fated oneness in submission,
Their duel — and their fateful dole.

And of two hearts, the one that's purer
And fonder in their unequal strife,
The one in self-surrender truer,
Who feels in all apartness poorer, —
Alone must pine away in life.

1851-1852

The poem is addressed to his mistress, Eléna Alexándrova Denisyeva. They met in 1850. She died of consumption on August 4, 1864. This book of translations includes a few other poems composed in her name, namely, *How Cruelly We Love Our Own* (page 59), *Oh, Do Not Say He Loves Me* (page 66), *Last Love* (page 68), *She Sat Upon the Floor* (page 75), *The Storm Dies Down* (page 78), *All Day She Lay Unconscious* (page 79), *July 15, 1865* (page 82), and *On the Eve* (page 84) which was the anniversary of her death. Their love was a source of great suffering to both, but the children were accepted by the family. However, Eléna died one year after her mother, also from consumption, at age 13; Nicholas died at age 1, and Fyodor in 1916 at the front, in his late fifties.

OH, DO NOT SAY HE LOVES ME

Oh, do not say he loves me now, the same
As in the days gone by, or cares for me!
Oh no! He's cruel, ruthless in his ways
And day by day he kills me, inhumanly.

I rage, complain; I cry out in my grief;
I'm wounded to the quick by angry strife.
I suffer, I do not live! I live for him,
For him alone! . . . O what a bitter life!

He measures grudgingly the air I breathe
As one would treat a hateful enemy.
I hardly breathe, so great the hurt I bear,
And wish for death, — to set me quickly free.

1851-1852

WINTER IS A SLY MAGICIAN!

Winter is a sly magician!
By his spell the forest bound
Stands, — a wondrous apparition,
Mute, all moveless, in submission,
Sparkling white, without a sound.

By a wizard captivated
In a world of hoar and snow
Stands the forest, fascinated,
Like a giant subjugated
By the downy chains of snow.

When the winter sun is streaming
In brief rays on branch and spray,
The enchanted forest, dreaming,
Stands in silence, glowing, gleaming
In its blinding beauty gay.

1852

LAST LOVE

How tenderly in our life's decline
We love, oft to unreason given!
O shine, departing day! O shine
On my last love — my light at even!

Blue shadows cover half the sky.
The West glows dimmer, faintly gleaming.
Sweet evening, stay, too soon to die!
O linger, in thy magic dreaming!

Let blood flow slower, yet the heart
Grows ever fonder, grows more tender.
O last dear love, so brief, thou art
My bliss, my hopeless self-surrender!

1853

SUMMER OF 1854

O what a summer! Look, how fair!
It's simply, simply glorious!
And why, I ask, such magic, why
Such magic, really, all for us?

I gaze, uneasy, as I watch
This summer splendor, summer light:
Is someone mocking, poking fun,
And smiles at us in sheer delight?

It seems exactly like a smile
On a young woman's face, — not bold,
Seductive, — a smile of lips and eyes
That stirs the heart when one is old.

1854

OH, THESE BARREN VILLAGES

Oh, these barren villages,
Lowly, naked, hungering, —
Land of all the Russian people,
Patient and long-suffering!

Scornful alien minds will never
Feel their beauty, never guess
The pure light and spirit shining
Through their humble nakedness.

Like a slave too weary, burdened
By His cross, our Saviour trod
All thy fields and plains, O Russia,
Blessing thee in the name of God.

1855

OH, MY PROPHETIC SOUL!

Oh, my prophetic soul! Oh, heart
Trembling in fear and desolation
Upon the threshold of creation,
By dual forces torn apart!

Two alien worlds are yours by fate:
Your day — a fierce distempered feeling;
Your dream at night — a vague revealing
Of life divine and ultimate.

Though fateful passions will defeat
Your heart, tormented and unwary,
Your soul forever longs, like Mary,
To cleave unto our Saviour's feet.

1855

MY VOWS OF LOVE

My vows of love and all the fair
Dear hopes I had are fused in me
By faith in one aspiring prayer:
Endure, endure their memory!

1856

THE STAR OF FREEDOM

When will thy star, O Freedom, rise,
And when will flash thy golden light
For unawakened multitudes,
For dark, rude peoples of the night?

I know thy beams will drive foul mists
Afar and quicken our life again. . . .
But what of ancient galling wounds,
The scars of outrage, guilt, disdain,

Corruption, emptiness of mind?
And what of wrongs too long ignored?
What grace will heal, make whole our life?
Only the seamless robe of Christ our Lord.

1857

THERE IS A TIME IN AUTUMN

There is a time in autumn of the year,
A time of fleeting magic light,
When crystal clear the days appear
And bright with stars the sky of night.

Where sickles loudly rang, now dead
The fields lie empty, silent, cold;
Only a filmy cobweb thread
Across a furrow-bed shines gold.

The birds have fled; now desolate the air.
The pine trees dream of winter snows.
Warm tides of azure flow across the bare
And weary fields in deep repose.

1857

SHE SAT UPON THE FLOOR

She sat upon the floor and scanned
A pile of letters at her side.
She tore and flung the sheets away
Like ashes upon a lifeless tide.

She lingered, gazing in amazement
At words remembered in her mind
As souls might gaze from heights above
Upon their bodies left behind.

How much of life and love they held!
What unrewarding tides of sadness!
How much of bitterness and grief
And unreturning days of gladness!

I stood in silence, sad, beside
Myself with deep regret and woes,
And strangely grieved I felt as though
A spirit of dear love arose.

1858

LATE AUTUMN DAYS

Late autumn days reveal to me
The beauty of the Royal Garden
When, soft in twilight loveliness,
Half-shrouded in a drowsy mist,
White-winged spirits seem to lie
In silence on the lake's dull glass
Like tranquil shadows, gleaming white
And moveless in grey October air.

The shadows climb the royal stairs
Of Catherine's great palaces
And softly rest in twilight languor
Throughout the early evening hours.
But as the garden lanes grow dark,
Beneath a star there dimly shines
Like a memory of glory past,
Alone, the golden cupola.

1858

I THINK OF HER

I think of her and of days afar
That bright with fabled fancies are,
As when the morning sun is high,
Or when, at dawn, a silver star
Sinks gently in the azure sky.

I knew her thus when in her face
Her grace shone sweet — the secret grace
Of dusk before the sunset hours
When, soft, unseen, the dews in space
Fall damp, unheard, among the flowers.

I think of her, and I recall
A life so perfect, a life withal
Above our earthly fret so far,
It seems she never died at all
But only set — as does a star.

1861

It is not known for certain to whom Tyutchev addressed this poem, but it is generally held he had in mind the queen dowager Alexandra Fyodorovna, wife of Tsar Nicholas I, a woman of uncommon grace and charm.

THE STORM DIES DOWN

The storm dies down. The surf of blue
Geneva's waters lies in calm.
Again the little sails flash by
And swans bestir the rippling glass.

Daylong, as though in summer heat,
The bright trees glisten in the sun,
And tenderly the gentle breezes
Caress the frail late autumn leaves.

Afar in space, in light serene,
Eternal in the cloudless sky,
Like an unearthly revelation
Shines lone, in solitude, Mont Blanc.

I might now feel its healing force
And forget the burden of the grief
I bear alone, were there at home
Among the graves one grave the less.

1864

ALL DAY SHE LAY UNCONSCIOUS

All day she lay unconscious, in a dream,
As evening shadows gathered at her side.
The summer rain came down, a warm soft stream,
And gaily rippled in the leaves outside.

Then slowly she awakened, with a sigh,
And listened to the sounds with grave elation.
She listened long as though enraptured by
A voice, her mind in conscious meditation.

And then, as though unto herself alone,
She murmured, remembering her life apart,
While I beside her stood all turned to stone:
"Oh, how I loved it all — with all my heart!"

How well you loved, how well! No one alive,
No one, could give, and give as you did give!
O God! . . . And would you die, while I survive
In all the world alone, — alone to live?

1864

O SEA OF NIGHT

Oh, thou art wondrous, O Sea of night,
Shining around me, dark-heaving in blue
Far-away space, and beneath the moon's light
Rolling, deep-throated, boundless in view!

Motion and thunder and splendor on high
Here in thy infinite freedom unite!
Gleaming with stars of the luminous sky,
Oh, thou art wondrous, alone in thy might!

Splendid, O Sea, in thy billowing race,
Speak, of what glory and triumph thy song?
Waves in great multitudes thunder apace
Golden with crystalline starshine nightlong.

Lulled by thy motion and musing in wonder,
Lonely I dream in my deep desolation.
Sweep me away, I pray, in thy thunder,
Cradled, O Sea, in thy vast fascination!

1865

SWEET MUSIC DWELLS
IN OCEAN WAVES

Est et arundineis
modulatio musica ripis.
– AUSONIUS

Sweet music dwells in ocean waves
And harmony in Nature's deeds
And strife; a rhythmic whisper flows,
Trembling, across the rustling reeds.

There is order in the world of Nature
And consonance on land and sea,
But men in all their phantom freedom
Are with Nature not in harmony.

Whence came our discords in the world?
Where now, in Nature's choir, the breed
Of men who sing as sings the sea?
Why still complains the *thinking reed*?

Between the earth and starry heavens,
Unanswered, in the empty air,
The soul's complaint in desert places,
The spirit's protest of despair!

1865

The phrase *thinking reed* was borrowed from Blaise Pascal's
Pensées: "L'homme n'est qu'un roseau le plus faible de la nature,
mais c'est un roseau pensant." The epigraph is from a fourth
century Latin poet, Decimus Magnus Ausonius, born 310 A.D.
(Man is no more than the weakest reed in nature, said Pascal,
but he is the thinking reed.)

JULY 15, 1865

This day, now fifteen years ago, was fated
To be for us a day of bliss divine
When you in all completeness then had mated
Your deepest spirit, one and whole, with mine.

Your life is over. No word of blame was spoken,
Yet all is lost. Alone I meet my doom.
I dread these days of loneliness unbroken,
And loneliness awaits me in the tomb.

1865

SUNRISE

The Eastern sky, uncertain, waits
In stillness sensitive and deep:
Is it the dawn, or wakeful sleep?
Is day outside the purple gates?

The mountain peaks gleam pale and mauve;
Grey mists over woods and valleys creep;
At peace, the towns and hamlets sleep.
Oh, lift your eyes to skies above!

Look there! A trembling bar of light
Now, as with secret passion fed,
Grows softer, brighter, deeper red,
Then flames, at the horizon, bright.

A moment longer, and anon
All measureless on land and sea
Will ring through all infinity
The triumph of the day and sun.

1865

ON THE EVE

Lone I rove the highway in my sorrow,
Silent in the waning light of day, —
Faint at heart, weary with every morrow,
Dearest, do you see me here, I pray?

Darker, gloomier the world around me
And my days in darkness disappear.
In a world where love for you has bound me,
Speak, my angel, do you see me here?

Morning brings the day of grief and sighing;
Morning marks that fateful day I've known.
Angel mine, where'er your soul is flying,
Dearest, do you see me here, alone?

August 3, 1865

THE SKY OF NIGHT

The sky of night is wrathful
With vapors shrouded deep;
No thought — a silence brooding
In gulfs of dull, dead sleep.
With tongues of sudden flashes
Through dark the lightning flares
As though the deaf-mute demons
Confer in demon lairs.

Then, at a common signal,
The sky with flame is bright;
Long fields and forest ranges
Shine vast within the night.
Then dark again and stillness
Deep in the trembling gloom:
It seems celestial councils
Ponder some secret doom.

1865

NEVER A DAY

Never a day but in my heart
I suffered, longing for the past.
I withered, grieving for a sign
Day after day, unto the last, —

In vain. I grieved as one who pines
With longing for his native land,
Who knows at last he's in his grave —
A grave within the deep sea sand.

1865

WHEN WE GROW OLD

When we grow old in mind and body
And fear we're losers in the race,
Or when, as the aged holding power,
We deny to younger men their place,

I pray we'll keep ourselves untainted
By spiteful censure, petty strife,
Ill temper, and exasperation
At changes in our changing life,

By sentiments of secret malice
Against the new and the untried
When round the festive board forgather
New leaders in their youthful pride;

By fretful, rankling apprehension
At being stranded, left behind,
When others with a sense of mission
Reflect afresh the social mind;

By grudges, by affronts we've hoarded
For years in secret, and, above
All else, by old men's peevish passions
More shameful than their senile love.

1866

RUSSIA

Russia's not fathomed by the mind,
Nor by some common standard known:
She is unique in all mankind;
Her fate, revealed through faith alone.

1866

O RUSSIAN STAR

How long wilt thou in hiding stay
Beyond a mist, O Russian Star?
Art thou a phantom of the air
Forever mocking from afar?

Or must our longing eyes, that watch
In darkness still to see thee rise,
Behold thee like a blaze of light
That faded in the empty skies?

The gloom is deeper, dread with grief,
And danger looms with threats of war:
Whose banner sinks upon the waves?
Awake! Rise now, or nevermore!

1866

HOWEVER DARK THE FINAL HOUR

However dark the final hour may be, —
That weary hour of mortal suffering
All dread, all desolate, past finding out,
It is more dreadful for the soul to see
That its best memories are dying out.

1867

FIRES

Far off and deep in space,
Compact, — thick clouds of smoke:
Abysmal, dense, they hide
The earth in columned dark.

The grass, the thickets smoulder;
The copse lies thin and flat;
Charred pines and spruces rim
The edges of the sky.

Thick smoke, no sparks ablaze
Across the burnt-out places:
Where now the dreadful flame,
That sovereign absolute?

Here, there the beast flares red
In secret, underhanded,
Like a live flame among
The bushes and the grass.

At twilight, sheets of smoke
Compound as one with darkness;
Their fitful sportive lights
And bonfires dot the camp.

How vast the ravage, wrath,
And ruin of fires! Poor man,
In silence, slack and weak,
Stands like a child in fear.

1868

CLOUDS FORM AND MELT

Clouds form and melt in space.
Flashing, in summer heat,
Glints of the river's steel
Run glowing adown the flood.

The heat grows denser; shades
Retreat among cool groves.
The breath of hay and honey
Waves in the sunlit fields.

What magic! . . . Through future ages
Again the summer heat,
The changeless river glints,
And the scent of meadowlands.

1868

NATURE IS A SPHINX

Nature is a sphinx. If the death of man
Bespeaks her proofs, her true reality,
She is then perhaps no living mystery
And never has been since the world began.

1869

TO MY BROTHER

Dear brother, best of all my friends,
Like you, I go to meet my death
Alone — in emptiness, — alone
Upon a vast and barren heath.

There now I wait. And yet how long?
Day follows day, but, fathomless,
The darkness gathers at my feet.
I stand, one lost in emptiness,

Where not a trace of conscious life
Survives, where all at last seems vain
Save for the howling winter storm,
The darkness, and the empty plain.

My days are brief, the past I loved
Too poor for grief; the future, stern
And dark, as I in darkness here
Alone must await my fated turn.

1870

WHAT HERITAGE IS OURS?

What good remains of life and struggles past
And all the sacrifices made in blood
These many years? What heritage is ours?
A barrow here and there, but nothing more,

An oaktree here and there among the graves.
These oaks, resounding far, survive in grace
And daring on the plain: They little care
Whose dust, whose memories their roots disturb.

Our phantom years are vain in Nature's scheme,
And all the same — all one — our living past.
We vaguely feel we are ourselves her dream,
Illusions all, — in emptiness conceived.

Thus, one by one, we come and go. In vain
Our excellence of mind, in vain our work.
She welcomes all, indifferent, in life
And death, into her all-embracing chasm.

1871

THE LORD TOOK
EVERYTHING AWAY

The Lord took everything away from me:
My will, my health, my rest, my breath of air.
You only has He left to care for me
That I could pray to Him in my despair.

1873

The poem is addressed to the poet's wife, Ernestine (née Pfeffel). They married in March, 1839. She was of an aristocratic Alsatian family, a titled widow of beauty and character. She was a woman of understanding, self-restraint and wonderful tact, who considered the welfare of the family above the poet's love affairs. Born in 1810, she outlived her husband by nearly twenty-one years. She learned Russian and took pride in editing the poet's collected works, — verse, letters, essays. Ernestine died on April 17, 1894.